This book belongs to

•••••••••••••••••••••

•••••••••••••••••••••

If you enjoy this book, please consider leaving
us a review by scanning the QR code below.
We are a small business but your review makes
a BIG difference!

thank you!

I SPY a red monster truck!
Can you find it?

That's correct!

How many monster trucks look like this one →

That's correct!
There are 3 of them.

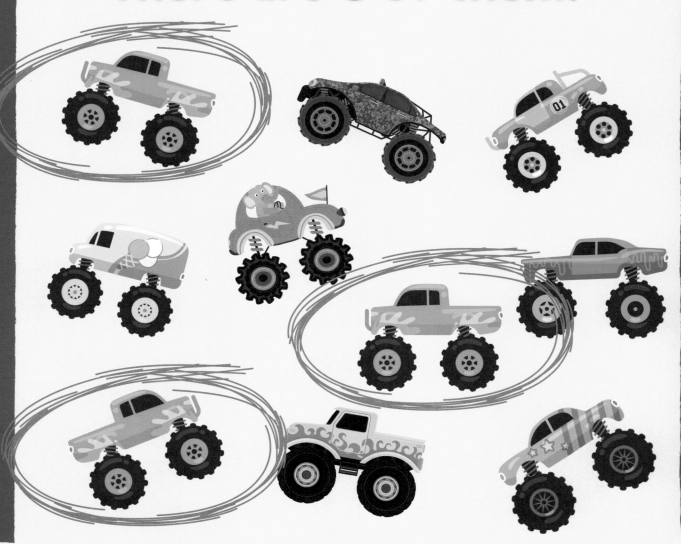

I SPY ice-cream trucks! How many are there?

That's correct!
There are 3 ice-cream
monster trucks.

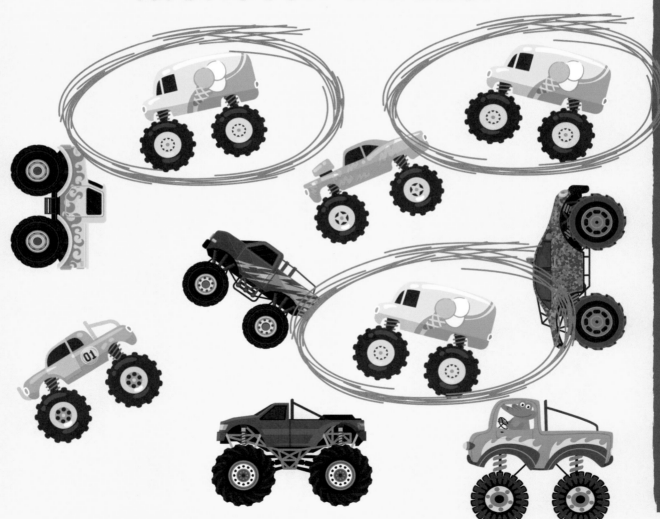

How many monster trucks have stars and stripes?

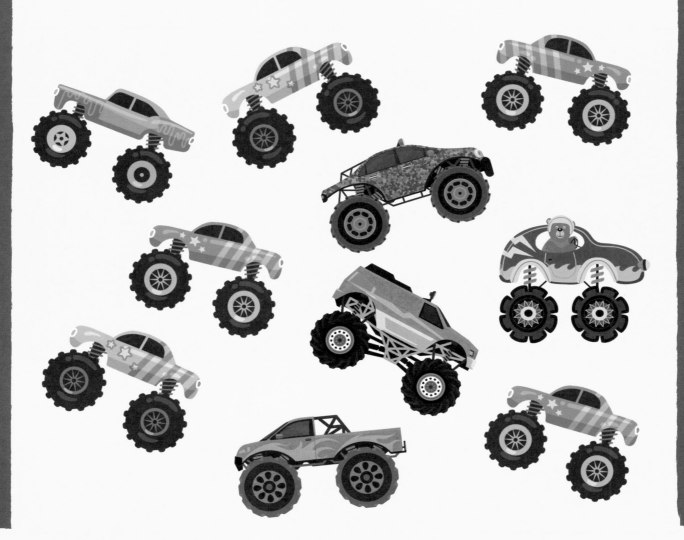

That's correct!
5 monster trucks have stars and stripes!

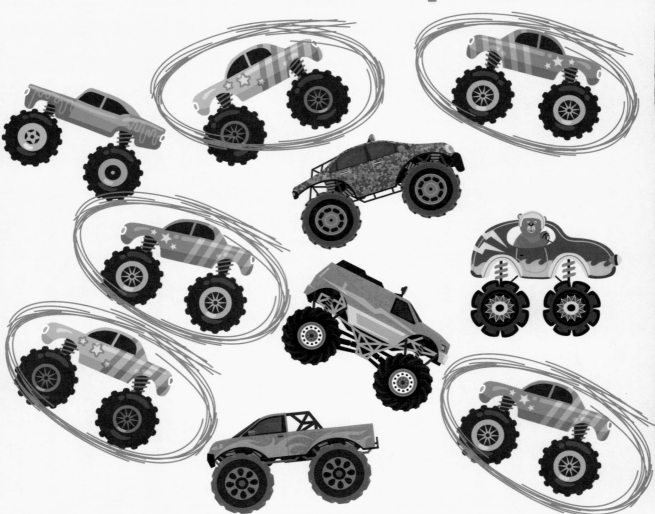

I SPY monster trucks that look the same!

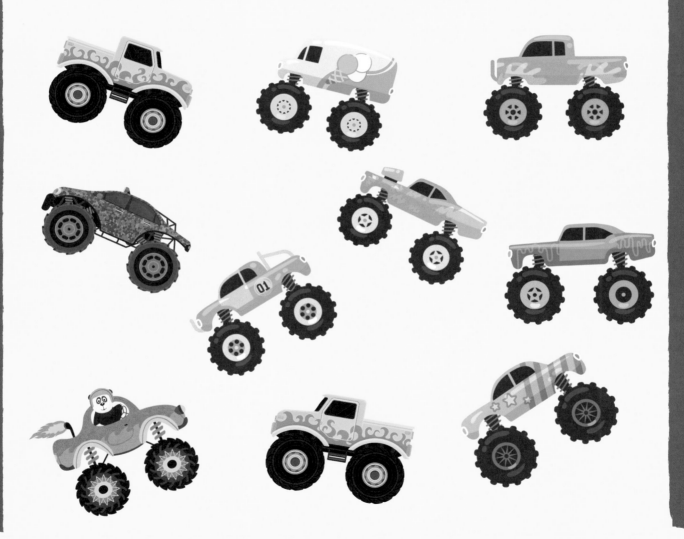

That's correct!
2 yellow monster trucks
look the same.

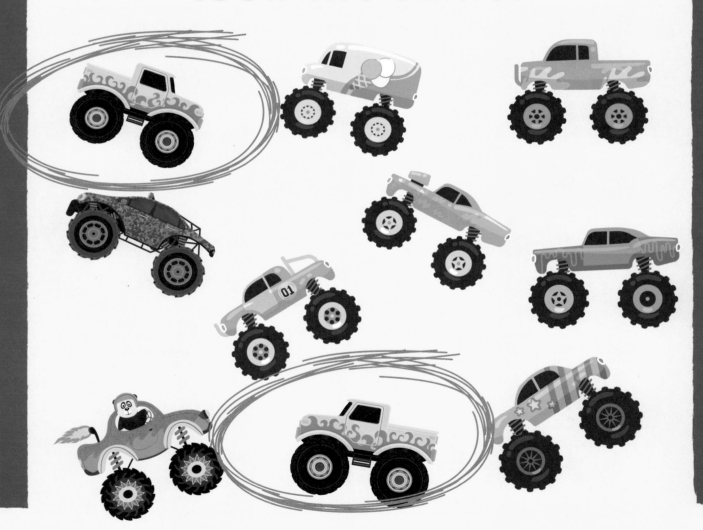

How many monster trucks look like this one →

That's correct!
There are 5 of them.

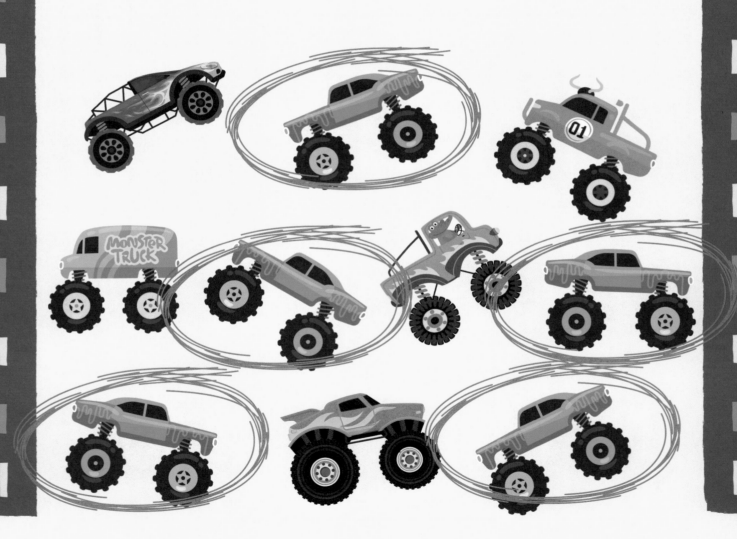

Count the yellow monster trucks!

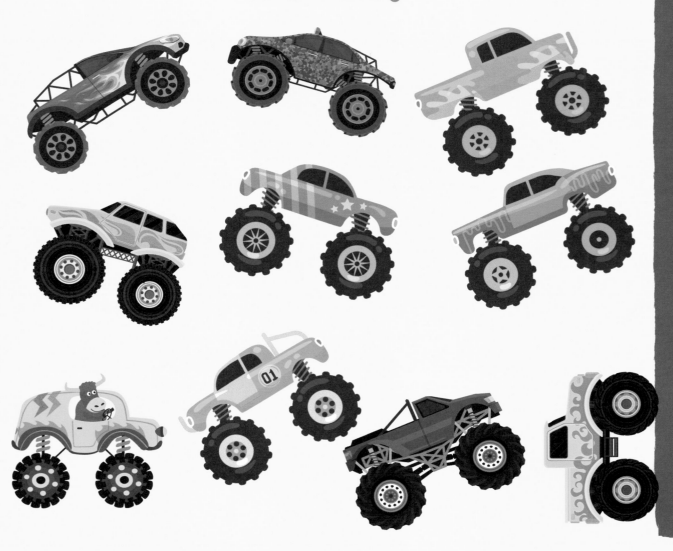

That's correct! There are 3 yellow monster trucks!

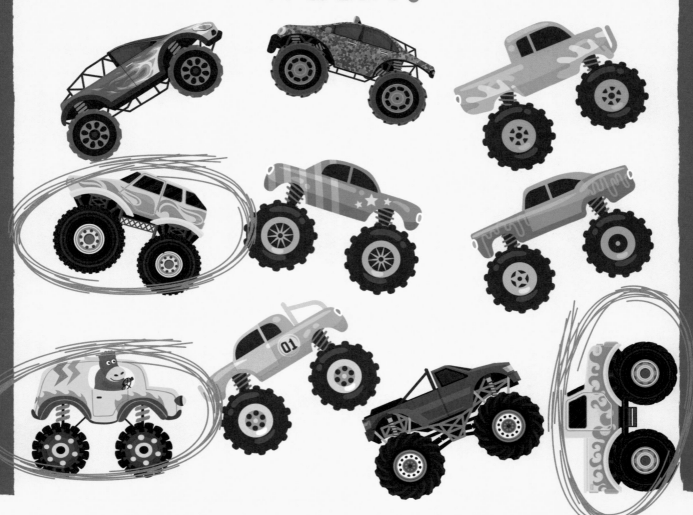

Can you see more elephants or zebras driving monster trucks?

That's correct!
More elephants are driving monster trucks than zebras.

How many monster trucks look like this one →

That's correct!
There are 4 of them.

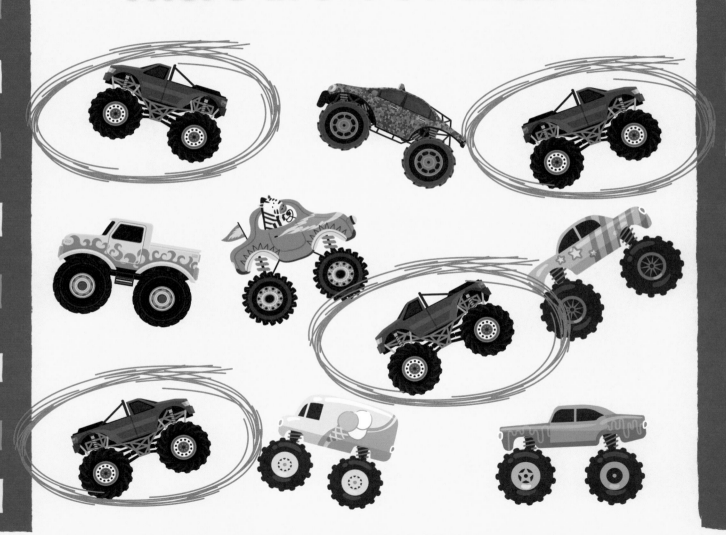

Are there more of these  or these  trucks?

That's correct! There are more of  than trucks.

How many monster trucks look like this one →

That's correct!
There are 2 of them.

I SPY a military monster truck! Can you find it?

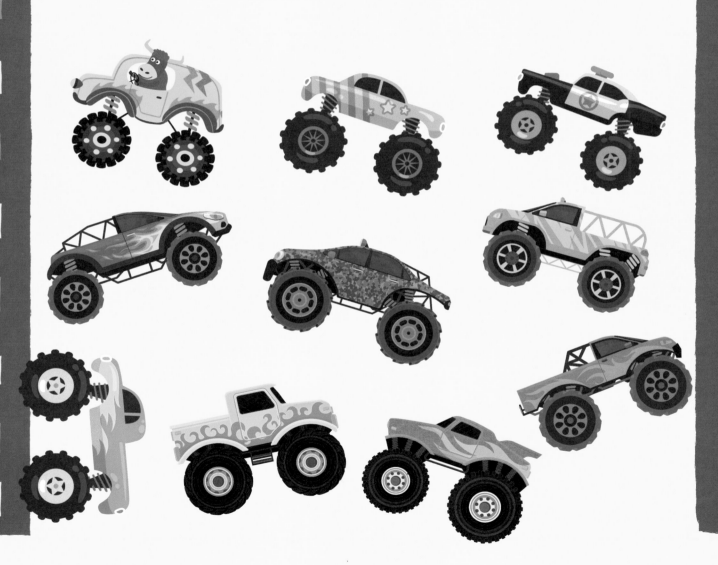

That's correct!
There is 1 military monster truck.

Are there more blue or pink monster trucks?

That's correct!
There are more **blue** monster trucks than **pink**!

How many monster trucks have yellow wheels?

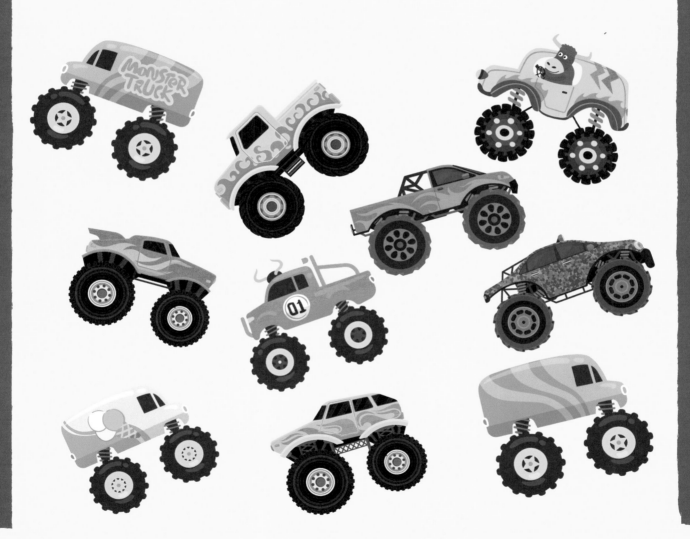

That's correct!
5 monster trucks have
yellow wheels!

How many monster trucks have tigers or crocodiles?

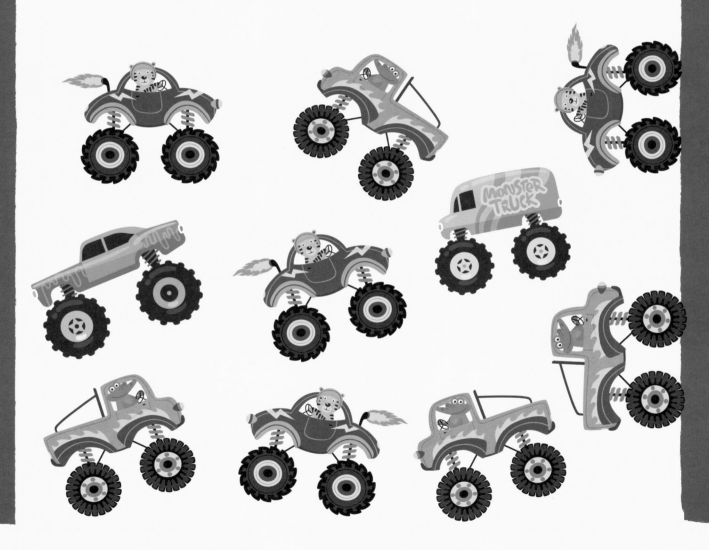

That's correct!
8 monster trucks have
tigers or crocodiles!

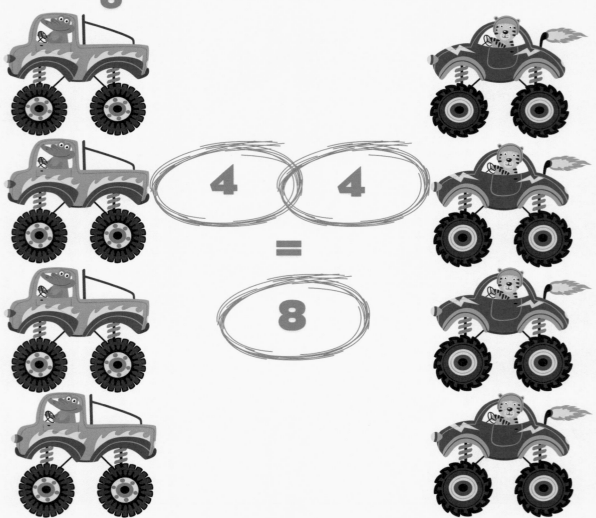

Count the blue monster trucks!

That's correct!
There are 5 blue monster trucks!

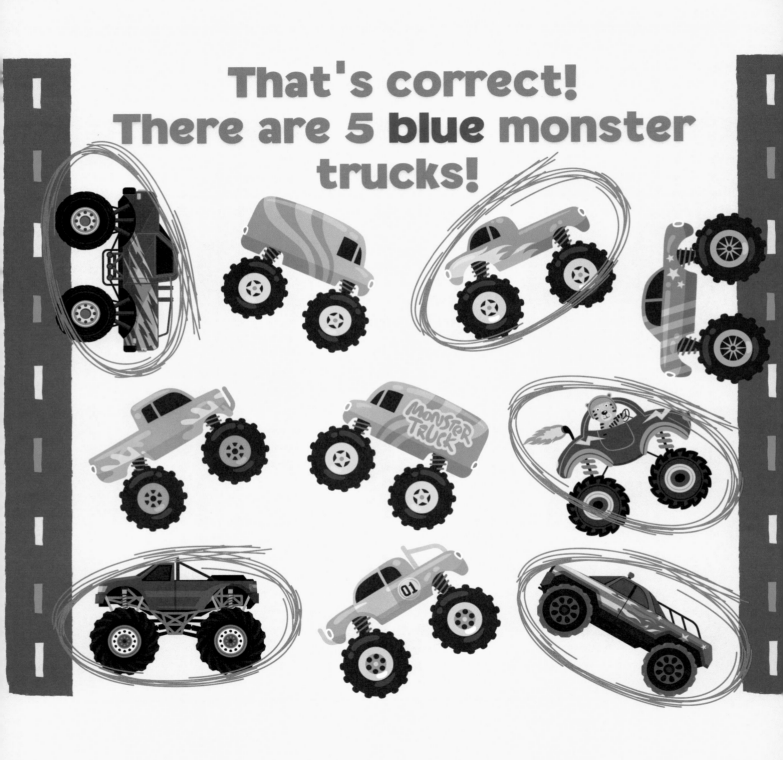

How many monster trucks have the number 01?

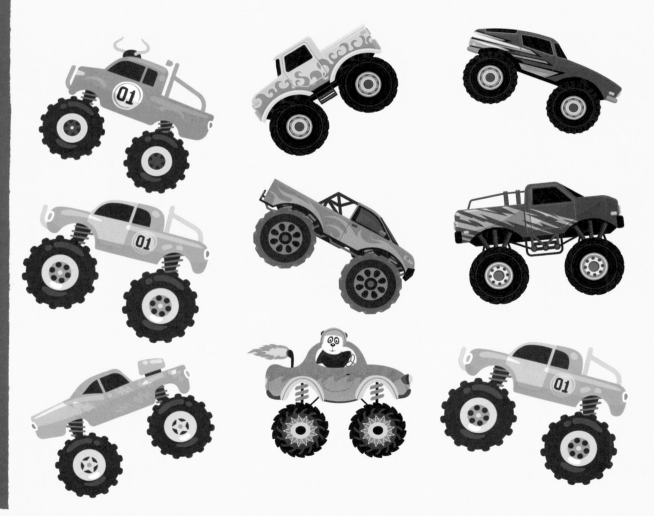

That's correct!
3 monster trucks have the number 01!

Count the police monster trucks!

That's correct!
There are 7 police monster trucks.

How many monster trucks have **blue** or green wheels?

That's correct!
5 monster trucks have
blue or green wheels!

Count the pink monster trucks!

That's correct!
There are 6 pink monster trucks!

Are there more green or orange monster trucks?

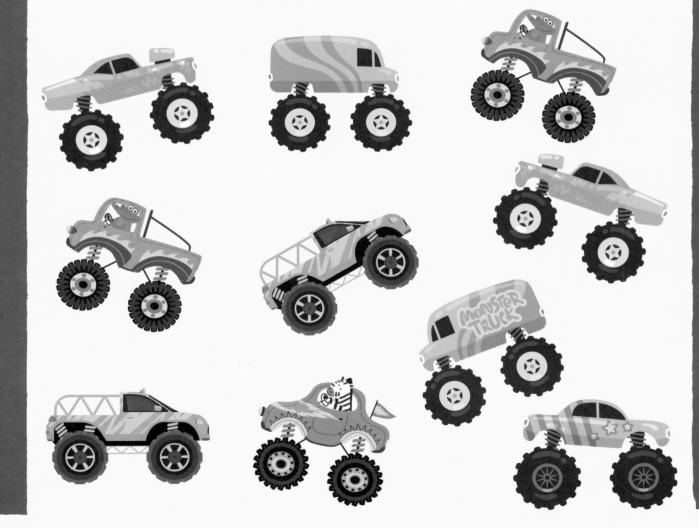

That's correct!
There are more orange monster trucks than green!

I SPY monster trucks with animals!
Can you count them?

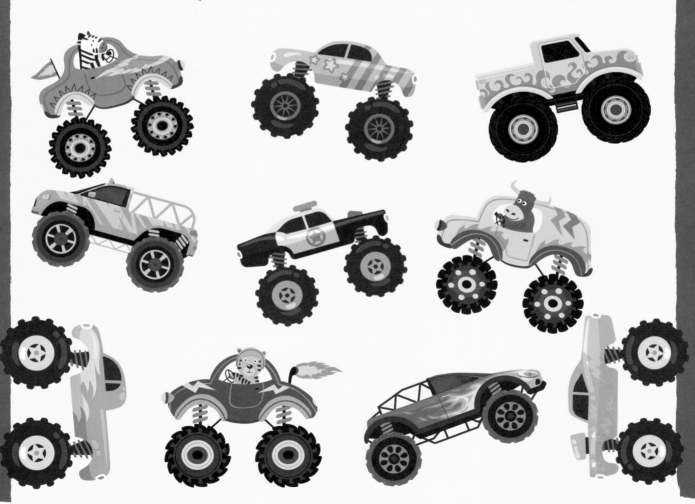

That's correct!
There are 3 monster trucks with animals.

Made in the USA
Columbia, SC
02 December 2023